D0578566

LOOKING AT
COUNTRIES

Looking at
GREAT BRITAIN

Jillian Powell

Gareth Stevens
Publishing

Please visit our web site at: www.garethstevens.com
For a free color catalog describing Gareth Stevens Publishing's list of
high-quality books, call 1-800-542-2595 (USA) or 1-800-387-3178 (Canada).

Library of Congress Cataloging-in-Publication Data

Powell, Jillian.
   Looking at Great Britain / Jillian Powell. — North American ed.
     p. cm. — (Looking at countries)
   First published: London : Franklin Watts, 2006.
   Includes index.
   ISBN: 978-0-8368-8170-7 (lib. bdg.)
   ISBN: 978-0-8368-8177-6 (softcover)
   1. Great Britain—Juvenile literature. I. Title.
DA27.5.P69 2007
941—dc22
                                      2007005948

_4348 4038 07/10_

This North American edition first published in 2008 by
Gareth Stevens Publishing
A Weekly Reader® Company
1 Reader's Digest Road
Pleasantville, NY 10570-7000 USA

This U.S. edition copyright © 2008 by Gareth Stevens, Inc.
Original edition copyright © 2006 by Franklin Watts.
First published in Great Britain in 2006 by Franklin Watts,
338 Euston Road, London NW1 3BH, United Kingdom

Series editor: Sarah Peutrill
Art director: Jonathan Hair
Design: Storeybooks Ltd.
Photo research: Diana Morris

Gareth Stevens managing editor: Valerie J. Weber
Gareth Stevens editors: Gini Holland and Dorothy L. Gibbs
Gareth Stevens art direction: Tammy West
Gareth Stevens graphic designer: Dave Kowalski

Photo credits: (t=top, b=bottom, l=left, r=right, c=center)
Sheila Attar/Cordaiy Photo. Library/Corbis: 18. Eleanor Bentall/Corbis: 21b. Martin Bond/Photofusion: 12,19t. Bryn Colton/Assignments
Photographers/Corbis: 20. Ashley Cooper/Corbis: 10, 17, 21t. Joe Cornish/National Trust Picture Library: 7b. Peter Dench/Corbis: 9t.
Adrian Don/Photographers Direct: 16. Robert Estall/Corbis: 9b. Malcolm Fife/zefa/Corbis: 19b. Paul Hardy/Corbis: cover, 27.
The Hoberman Collection/Alamy: 23b. Dewitt Jones/Corbis: 11. Gareth Wyn-Jones/Photofusion: 22. Ray Juno/Corbis: 6.
Gary Lee/UPPA/Topfoto: 25t. Tim MacMillan/Garden Picture Library/Alamy: 25b. Christine Osborne/Corbis: 13.
Robert Paterson/Reuters/Corbis: 24. Derry Robinson/National Trust Picture Library: 7t. Christa Stadtler/Photofusion: 23t.
Superbild/A1 Pix: 26b. Sandro Vianni/Corbis: 4b. Patrick Ward/Corbis: 8. Josh Westrick/zefa/Corbis: 26t. Adam Woolfitt/Corbis: 14,
title page, 15.

Every effort has been made to trace the copyright holders for the photos used in this book. The publisher apologizes,
in advance, for any unintentional omissions and would be pleased to insert the appropriate acknowledgements in any
subsequent edition of this publication.

Printed in the United States of America

1 2 3 4 5 6 7 8 9 11 10 09 08 07

Contents

Words that appear in the glossary are printed in **boldface** type the first time they occur in the text.

Where Is Great Britain?

Great Britain is an island made up of three countries: England, Scotland, and Wales. It is in western Europe.

London is the capital city of both England and the United Kingdom. Edinburgh is the capital of Scotland, and Cardiff is the capital of Wales. Britain has many historic buildings, including fine houses, castles, and cathedrals.

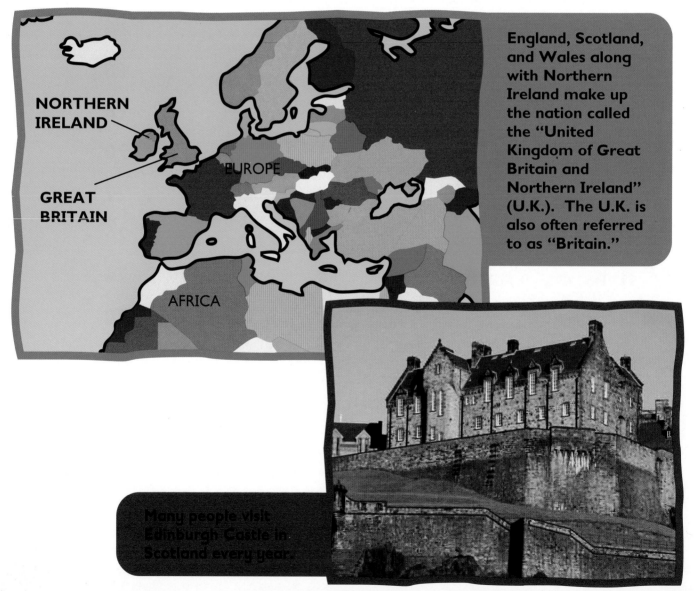

NORTHERN IRELAND

EUROPE

GREAT BRITAIN

AFRICA

England, Scotland, and Wales along with Northern Ireland make up the nation called the "United Kingdom of Great Britain and Northern Ireland" (U.K.). The U.K. is also often referred to as "Britain."

Many people visit Edinburgh Castle in Scotland every year.

Great Britain has a coastline along the Atlantic Ocean in the west and the North Sea in the east. The Irish Sea lies between Ireland and Great Britain. The English Channel is between France and Great Britain.

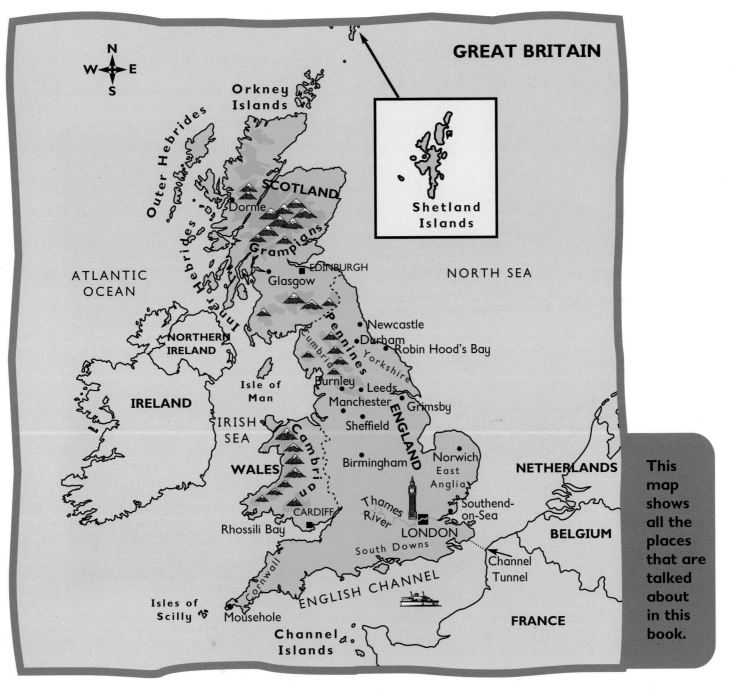

This map shows all the places that are talked about in this book.

The Landscape

Great Britain has many kinds of landscapes. Northern England, Scotland, and Wales have the highest mountains. The north is also home to many lakes and large moors, or high, open land. Sheep graze on the moors.

Eilean Donan castle stands on the western coast of Scotland, near the village of Dornie. It rests on a small island where three *lochs* — the Scottish word for "lakes" — meet.

Grasses and wildflowers grow on the South Downs.

Most of Great Britain's good crop land lies in the gentle hills along the middle and south of the island. The grasslands of the hilly Downs cover much of the far south. Great Britain's coastline changes from rugged, rocky cliffs in the west to the wide, sandy beaches of East Anglia.

Robin Hood's Bay, which is in northeastern England, is famous for the rock pools on its beach.

Weather and Seasons

Great Britain has a mild climate with warm summers and cool winters. Scotland and northern England have the coldest winters, with snow on the mountains and hills.

Winter snow falls most often on higher ground such as on these North York Moors in Yorkshire.

Even rain cannot keep people from visiting the beach in summer at Southend-on-Sea in southeastern England.

Heavy rains can sometimes make rivers flood in winter. The warm summer months can somtimes bring **droughts**, although it usually rains year-round.

The south is the sunniest part of the country. In the southwest and the Isles of Scilly, the warm **Gulf Stream** from the Atlantic Ocean causes mild winters, allowing even **subtropical** plants to grow.

Did you know?

The Lake District in Cumbria in the north is the rainiest part of England.

Summer sunshine bathes the golden sands of Rhossili Bay in Wales.

British People

People have lived in Great Britain for thousands of years. People have also moved there from many other areas, including India, Pakistan, China, the Caribbean, and African countries. Many groups have settled in big cities such as London, Birmingham, and Manchester.

Did you know?

The Notting Hill Carnival in London celebrates Caribbean culture each year.

This food store in Burnley in northern England is in an area with a large Asian community.

This man is showing off two symbols of Scotland — highland cattle and the kilt. The kilt is a skirt for men and part of the traditional outfit for Scots.

Christianity is the main religion in Great Britain. Most Christians belong to the Protestant Church of England or Scotland, but Great Britain is also home to many Roman Catholics. Large communities of Muslims, **Hindus**, **Sikhs** (said like *SEEKS*), and Jews live there as well.

English is the main language, although people have many different **accents** and **dialects**. Welsh, Gaelic, Punjabi, Hindi, and Urdu are also spoken in Britain.

School and Family

Family life in Great Britain has changed in recent times. Many children now live with one-parent families or with stepfamilies. Relatives sometimes live far apart and get together only for special family occasions, such as weddings or funerals.

These city families found a way to have some fun at the "beach" without leaving town!

Children wearing their school uniforms sing at morning assembly at a primary school in London.

Children in Great Britain usually start school when they are five years old. Many start earlier or go to day care or babysitters if both parents are working.

School days usually start at 9 a.m. and end at 3:30 p.m. Children whose parents work may go to after-school clubs for sports and other activities.

Did you know?

In parts of Wales, school is taught in the Welsh language.

Country Life

This is a traditional cream tea, or afternoon tea served with rolls, cream, and jam. Here, it is served in a farmer's garden tea shop.

Only one of every ten people in Great Britain live in the countryside. Many people live in towns and cities because these places have more jobs.

About three-fourths of Great Britain's countryside is farmland. Some farmers have started businesses, such as stores that sell food made from farm crops. Some allow people to tour the farms and pet the animals. Farmers sometimes also use their farm buildings for other industries, including producing pottery and weavings.

Mousehole is a typical fishing village in Cornwall. Many people have vacation homes there.

Most country people live in villages or market towns that have a church, small stores, and a **pub**, or bar. Country people can also shop at large stores in nearby cities. Some city people have second homes or vacation homes in country towns.

Did you know?

Most of Great Britain was once covered with forests and woodlands.

City Life

Most people live in towns or cities. London is the largest city in Great Britain. More than seven million people live there. Birmingham, Leeds, and Glasgow are the next largest cities.

The Quayside and Millennium Bridge are part of the new waterfront walkways of Newcastle.

Many British cities, such as Durham and Norwich, have old cathedrals, churches, castles, and houses. Some cities have recently **redeveloped** their older sections, especially areas along rivers and **canals**.

More than one million people travel into London each day by a system of underground trains. This system is called "the tube."

Did you know?

Birmingham has more canals than Venice, Italy.

Traffic is often a problem on Great Britain's busy roads. Most people in London and Glasgow travel on underground trains. People in Birmingham, Manchester, and Sheffield use streetcars and buses.

British Houses

Great Britain has many kinds of houses. In the countryside, many old houses and cottages are built from stone. Some houses have **thatched** or tiled roofs. New houses on the edges of towns are often built in these same traditional styles.

Many thatched cottages in British villages are more than five hundred years old.

The largest houses in Great Britain are stately historic homes. Many are now open to the public as tourist attractions. Some offer tours of their gardens and provide tea shops for visitors.

These terrace houses in Manchester were built more than one hundred years ago.

Glasgow is known for tall apartment buildings like this one. In recent years, some shorter apartment buildings have been built to replace many of them.

In Great Britain's cities, many people live in apartments or terraces. Terraces are rows of houses that look alike, with shared walls between them. Some are new. Others are over one hundred years old.

British Food

Many British people shop for their food in supermarkets. Most towns and cities also have market squares or street markets where people shop daily for fresh foods.

Norwich, in Norfolk, has had an outdoor market for about eight hundred years.

Traditional British dishes include roast beef with potatoes and vegetables. Another favorite is a cooked breakfast of bacon, eggs, and fried tomatoes.

Did you know?

Great Britain once ruled India, and Indian foods are now very popular in Britain.

This man sells local cheeses in a booth at a country fair.

Some dishes, such as **Yorkshire pudding** and **Cornish pasties**, came from particular areas, but people all over Great Britain eat them. Haggis, traditionally made from a mixture of oats and meat from sheep, is the national dish of Scotland. The Scots cook the mixture inside a stomach from a sheep! Great Britain is famous for its cheeses, such as cheddar and Stilton.

Britain's most popular dish is spicy Indian curry made with meat or vegetables. Burgers, fried chicken, and Chinese and Italian foods are also favorites.

Fish-and-chips, wrapped in paper, is a traditional British take-out meal.

At Work

Great Britain's main industries include manufacturing of machine tools, processed foods, and clothes. Many British work in the aircraft industry and in car assembly for Japanese-owned factories.

These men are preparing fish at a factory in Grimsby on the northeastern coast.

This math teacher is helping students. Teaching is one of the most popular jobs in Great Britain.

Service industries, such as banking and working in hotels, have grown quickly in Great Britain. Many people work in offices, stores, schools, or hospitals.

These police officers are on duty at Buckingham Palace, which is the queen's house in London.

Having Fun

Tennis, soccer, cricket, and rugby are all popular sports in Great Britain, where soccer is called football. During the football season, many fans come to watch their teams play. The final soccer game of the season is the Football Association (FA) Cup.

Did you know?

Watching television is Britain's favorite fun activity.

Celtic fans cheer their soccer team as they compete in a Scottish Premier League game.

Christmas and Easter are important Christian holidays. Many people celebrate by going to church and gathering for special meals with their families. Many other British people celebrate Hindu festivals, such as Holi and **Diwali**, or Muslim festivals, such as Eid al-Fitr.

Pantomimes are traditional Christmas shows with songs and dances based on fairy-tale stories and characters.

Many other events, such as country fairs and festivals, are held around the country during the warmer summer months.

Gardening is very popular in Britain. These people are at the Chelsea Flower Show, which is held every year in London.

Britain: The Facts

• Great Britain, as part of the United Kingdom (U.K.), is a member of the **European Union**. The queen is **head of state**. The prime minister leads the government.

• Great Britain has eighty-six regions, called counties, and more than six hundred districts. Each district elects its own **member of Parliament** (MP).

The British currency is the pound. All coins and paper money have a picture of the queen on them.

The United Kingdom flag, called the Union Jack, combines the crosses of the patron saints of England, Ireland, and Scotland.

Did you know?

Big Ben is the name of the bell inside the clock tower of the Houses of **Parliament**.

**The London Eye is a giant Ferris wheel.
It is a new landmark on the Thames River.**

• About fifty-nine million people live in Great Britain. As part of the U.K., Great Britain also has a number of lands besides the island itself. These include the Channel Islands, Bermuda (a group of islands in the Atlantic Ocean off the coast of the United States), and Gibraltar (next to the southern coast of Spain).

• Great Britain's capital, London has many grand old buildings, parks, museums, and art galleries. New landmarks, such as the Millennium Bridge and the London Eye, attract visitors from all over the world.

Glossary

accents — the ways people from different areas say words

canals — waterways made for boats to carry goods

Cornish pasties — kinds of pies that come from Cornwall. These pastries are filled with meat and vegetables.

dialects — different ways of speaking a language

Diwali — (said like *dee-VAHL-ee*) the Hindu Festival of Lights, held in late October or early November

downs — areas of rolling, mainly treeless, grassy land

droughts — long periods of time with little or no rain

European Union — a group of countries in western Europe that have joined together to share trade, laws, and, if they choose to, a single currency (the Euro)

Gulf Stream — a warm current in the North Atlantic Ocean

head of state — the person who represents a country

Hindus — people who practice the Hindu religion, worshipping the divine in the forms of many gods and goddesses

member of Parliament — someone who is elected by the people in a district to represent them in Parliament

Parliament — the place where the people's representatives make laws

patron saints — persons who are believed to represent a country or person in heaven

pub — a public place where people can buy alcoholic drinks

redeveloped — rebuilt buildings and improved land

semidetached — refers to a pair of houses that are built with a shared wall between them

service industries — businesses that serve people but not businesses that make objects

Sikhs (said like *SEEKS*) — people who follow the Sikh religion and worship one God

subtropical — relating to land near the Tropics and describing areas that are wet and warm and the plants that grow there

thatched — made of straw or other dried grass

traditional — describes ways and beliefs that have been passed down thorough a group of people for many years

Yorkshire pudding — a baked side dish first made in Yorkshire

Find Out More

British Government Page for Kids
www.BritainUSA.com/4Kids

Wild Life in Great Britain
www.bbc.co.uk/nature/reallywild/features/holiday_guide/
  great_britain.shtml

Time for Kids: Britain
www.timeforkids.com/TFK/hh/goplaces/main/0,20344,604850,
00.html

Publisher's note to educators and parents: Our editors have carefully reviewed these Web sites to ensure that they are suitable for children. Many Web sites change frequently, however, and we cannot guarantee that a site's future contents will continue to meet our high standards of quality and educational value. Be advised that children should be closely supervised whenever they access the Internet.

My Map of Great Britain

Photocopy or trace the map on page 31. Then write in the names of the countries, cities and towns, bodies of water, and regions listed below. (Look at the map on page 5 if you need help.)

After you have written in the names of all the places, find some crayons and color the map!

Countries
France
Northern Ireland
Ireland
Scotland
Wales

Bodies of Water
Atlantic Ocean
English Channel
Irish Sea
North Sea
Thames River

Regions
Cornwall
Cumbria
East Anglia
Rhossili Bay
South Downs
Yorkshire

Cities and Towns
Birmingham
Burnley
Cardiff
Dornie
Durham
Edinburgh
Glasgow
Grimsby
Leeds
London
Manchester
Mousehole
Newcastle
Norwich
Robin Hood's Bay
Sheffield
Southend-on-Sea

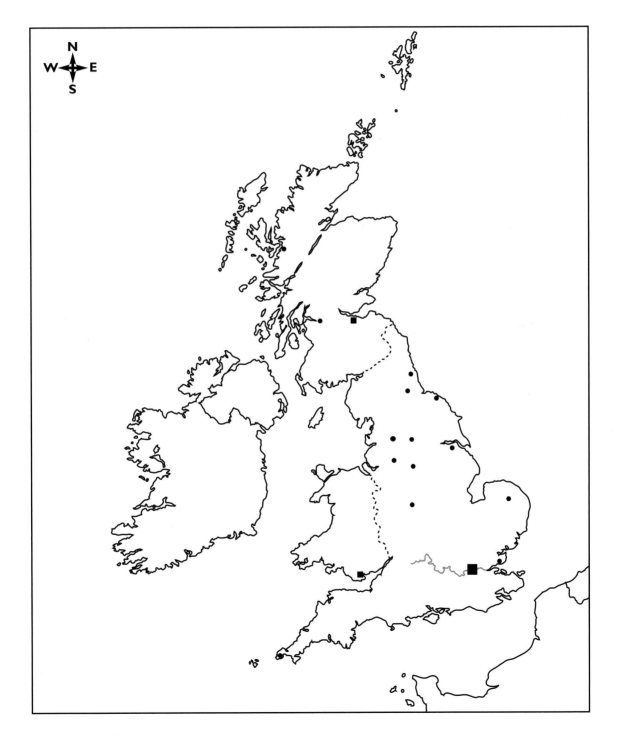

31

Index